Big Dump Trucks

Amy Hayes

Cavendish Square

New York

Published in 2016 by Cavendish Square Publishing, LLC
243 5th Avenue, Suite 136, New York, NY 10016

Copyright © 2016 by Cavendish Square Publishing, LLC

First Edition

CPSIA Compliance Information: Batch #WS15CSQ

All websites were available and accurate when this book was sent to press.

Library of Congress Cataloging-in-Publication Data

Hayes, Amy.
Big dump trucks / Amy Hayes.
pages cm. — (Machines that work)
Includes index.
ISBN 978-1-50260-395-1 (hardcover) ISBN 978-1-50260-394-4 (paperback) ISBN 978-1-50260-396-8 (ebook)
1. Dump trucks—Juvenile literature. I. Title.

TL230.15.H39 2016
629.224—dc23

2014050259

Editorial Director: David McNamara
Copy Editor: Cynthia Roby
Art Director: Jeffrey Talbot
Designer: Stephanie Flecha
Senior Production Manager: Jennifer Ryder-Talbot
Production Editor: Renni Johnson

The photographs in this book are used by permission and through the courtesy of: Per-Anders Pettersson/Photonica World/Getty Images, cover; © iStockphoto.com/Skyhobo, 5; David Wall Photo/Lonely Planet Images/Getty Images, 7; John W Banagan/Photographer's Choice/Getty Images, 9; Monty Rakusen/Cultura/Getty Images, 11; Lester Lefkowitz/The Image Bank/Getty Images, 13; breckeni/E+/Getty Images, 15; Faraways/Shutterstock, 17; © iStockphoto.com/Andyqwe, 19; Southern Stock/Digital Vision/Getty Images, 21.

Printed in the United States of America

Contents

Dump trucks are big trucks!

4

5

Dump trucks have big tires and carry heavy **loads**.

7

Dump trucks carry dirt.

8

9

Dump trucks carry rocks.

Dump trucks can **pour** out their loads.

13

They lift their **containers** high into the air.

14

The front of the dump truck is called the **cab**.

It is where the driver sits.

17

Dump trucks work with other big **machines**.

18

19

Dump trucks work hard
all day!

20

21

New Words

cab (CAB) The part of the truck in which the driver sits.

containers (kun-TANE-erz) Something into which other things can be put.

loads (LODES) A large mass that is carried.

machines (muh-SHEENS) Equipment with moving parts that are used to do jobs.

pour (PORE) To cause to flow out.

Index

About the Author

Amy Hayes lives in the beautiful city of Buffalo, New York. She has written several books for children, including the Machines That Work and the Our Holidays series for Cavendish Square.

About BOOKWORMS

Bookworms help independent readers gain reading confidence through high-frequency words, simple sentences, and strong picture/text support. Each book explores a concept that helps children relate what they read to the world in which they live.